MW00595955

Never Mind:

Letters I Will

Never Send

Volume 2:
Dear Mom

Kateri

https://kateriwritingllc.wordpress.com

ISBN: 978152824153

Dedication

I heard of a tradition by some that involves giving gifts to Mom on one's own birthday. After all, it was Mom who did all the real work on that day I came into the world. I was a big baby (9+ pounds), so in my case, Mom definitely deserves the accolades.

Besides this, I am who I am because of Mom. Whether through DNA, environment, or a little of both, I picked up many of her tendencies, habits, preferences, dispositions, and characteristics. After many years, I have finally come to like who I am, so I dedicate this work to you, Mom. Thanks for being you so that I can be me.

Contents

Acknowledgments

So many wonderful people have stood by me and offered encouragement and support for all the years it took me to figure out what I wanted to be when I grow up. I thrive when I have such thoughtful friends, relatives, students, and colleagues to share ideas with.

Thanks especially to Dee, Don, Jessica, Susan, Neha, Jay, Barb, and Steve for reading my writing and offering reflective, attentive, and constructive feedback.

And I appreciate all of the people behind the scenes that might be overlooked, such as the manuscript preparer, the logo designer, the cover formatter, and those who went before me in the world of authorship who offered valuable advice.

Much gratitude, also, to Cindy and Dave, who reaffirmed my faith in the kindness of strangers.

Thank you, all of you.

Introduction

What do you say to someone who has known you all your life? What do you say to someone to whom you owe nearly everything?

I wanted to include a letter to Mom in my second volume of *Never Mind: Letters I Will Never Send*, but I found that I had too much to say for just one letter. So this volume is actually a series of letters to my mom, which still doesn't include all that I would like to say to this very special woman.

I guess in any relationship, many things are left unsaid. These thoughts and memories, full of gratitude and reflection, are here for those interested in exploring the mother-daughter dynamic and those interested in examining who they are and why. These letters may evoke fond remembrances. They may induce laughter, or heavy sighing, or wonder. Maybe even awe. I enjoyed moving back through my life and thinking about who I am and why. I savored processing all the things that happened to me, how I reacted, and what I learned.

Mom and Dad raised four strong, unique individuals, which is a testament to their exceptional ability to encourage and support each of our separate paths. As I wrote this, it became more and more evident that the more I try to understand Mom, the closer I come to understanding myself and the path that I am on.

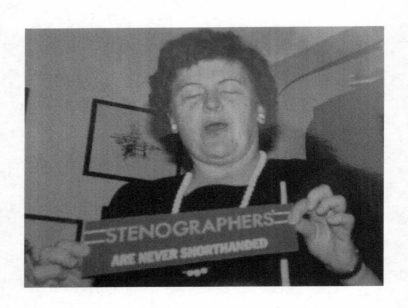

1 – Working

Dear Mom,

For as long as I can remember, you had a job. Not all of my friends' moms did. Even though you had several different jobs through the years, I never got the impression that your skills would ever be less than in high demand. Every company needed secretaries and assistants. Every organization needed someone to type up the documents and spell check or file the forms. I don't know how we could have been able to afford Catholic education for four kids and a summer vacation every year without your contribution to the income. I remember you and dad carefully planning each day of each vacation, how far we will drive, where we will stay, what attractions we will enjoy. I recall discussions about prioritizing expenses and figuring out which car we could get or what home improvements we could afford.

Flexibility was built into all of this planning. You never know when someone like me might flatten two tires by driving too close to the curb. On a trip, we might see something interesting along a side road or someone might get sick. We almost met Hurricane Agnes in Florida and had to leave in a hurry. We got submarine sandwiches on the way out of town. I only ate half of mine. The next day I ate the other half. Since that sandwich had mayonnaise on it, I ended up throwing up for three days, so we stayed at a motel somewhere in Georgia. Sorry about that. It was many years before I could eat a sub again.

I learned from you that I should always have a plan B, and C, and D. Your example and the example of all of the women in our family who had to support themselves after the loss of a husband reinforced for me the need to be independent, especially financially. I have had a job in some form or another since I was 17 years old. I may very well continue working until I am 67, or maybe longer. Part of my thinking when deciding to go into teaching was noticing that I had many very old teachers. And, unlike a more physically demanding job, teaching is an occupation that can continue well into one's elder years. And apparently, longevity runs in our family, at least with the women.

That independence also showed its importance when dad died. Not only were you left to continue on your own financially, but some of the so-called friends that you and dad socialized with suddenly vanished. This sent a powerful message to me about true friendship and social independence. It's one thing to ask, "How is your mom?" at an accidental meeting in a coffee shop; it's quite another to actually call and set up some time to spend together.

Through your guidance and example, I learned to plan for independence and make sound decisions based on reality. When I was offered that job teaching French in Vermont, I first did all the figuring. After careful research, when I realized that I would actually lose money on the deal because of the cost of living, I declined this particular opportunity.

I inherited tendencies and preferences from you; one of them is happily letting the other guy be the life of the party. I think we are both better at being behind the scenes. The one who makes everything look like it's running smoothly so that the person on stage looks good. Many of the plays I participated in began with me in the role of stage manager or assistant director. Oddly, though, on several occasions, something happened to one of the actors and I ended up filling in, mostly because I had inadvertently memorized everyone's lines. I would help out, but, like you, I would prefer to have my husband or someone else engage in all that socially acceptable small talk and entertain the troops. Like you, I would prefer not to be in the spotlight. When my husband works the room, that takes the pressure off of me. I am more comfortable in the background. And it's just way easier for me to accurately gauge whether or not someone is out of ice than it is for me to determine whether or not someone else is having fun. Reading the room is not my strong suit. Neither is eye contact. Ironically, I discovered that acting in a play or even reading at church or facilitating learning in a classroom actually allowed me to hide behind another character. Hiding in plain sight. Encouraging and inspiring others to shine.

While you often let dad take the spotlight, it was obvious to me, and you must have known it, too, that in dad's eyes, there was no one more important, more special, more treasured than you, Joanie. You were the air in his whipped cream. You were the cherry on his sundae. He would do anything for you, even to the point of remodeling the basement, climbing up a ladder to clean out the gutter, or balancing precariously on the roof to install a new bathroom fan. He wanted to impress you and make you happy. He wanted to provide for you everything that you deserved. You told me once that you never had an issue with having to convince your husband to do something. Me neither.

I do remember, though, that dad never did the dishes. That was the one chore he avoided. I couldn't figure that one out at first. Then it occurred to me that his syringomyelia had progressed to the point where he had already lost feeling in at least one of his hands. I must conclude, then, that he didn't want to do the dishes because he didn't want to break anything.

Dad extended his desire to please to his kids, which may be why you often had to take on the part of the bad guy. He didn't like to say "no," so you had to be the one to lay down the law. Dad would, of course, back you up and enforce what you said. You both insisted that the decisions came from a consensus between you two. I have always believed this to be true. Nevertheless, for some reason, you always seemed to be the one who had to give us the bad news. I can relate to this, too. As a step-mother, I gracefully accepted that I would be the bad guy, the one to apply tough love. My husband, like my father, does not like to say "no." I was frequently the one who insisted the kids earned trust and fulfilled their obligations. Years later, I respect you for taking this more difficult route and showing me how to do the same.

Even in my classroom, I have learned that the work and preparation up front makes it a whole lot easier in the long run. Teaching responsibility takes a lot of initial effort and sometimes makes the teacher (or parent) look like the bad guy. But if I'm patient, I eventually reap the rewards when the students or step-children can achieve success and a personal sense of accomplishment without my help and constant reminders. An effective parent or teacher works to facilitate the development of a child or student who is independent and no longer needs oversight. We succeed when they don't need us anymore. Thank you for being the model for me.

Maybe it was because of your work schedule, but unlike me in those days, you went to bed earlier than anyone else and you were a very light sleeper. Waking you up seemed particularly unfair since you had to get to work in the morning. I had to figure out how to get from one end of the house to the other without disturbing you. I knew every step that was the least bit unstable or creaky. I could walk past dad asleep on his chair in the living room with no problem, but trying to get past the closed bedroom door without waking you up was quite the challenge. Sometimes I made it. Sometimes I didn't.

And being the night owl that I was, I spent many late hours reading under the blankets with a flashlight. I could occasionally read by the light of the lamp in the alley, or do homework that I had put off until bedtime. I did that quite often. I would much rather spend my evenings in the living room watching now classic cop shows, courtroom dramas, or mysteries with you and dad. You would be on the couch doing a crossword puzzle or filing your nails and dad would be in his chair reading a magazine or just predicting who committed the TV crime. I picked up that habit of constantly working on my nails. I have a nail file and cuticle scissors strategically placed in several places so that I do not have to go far in the event of a nail emergency.

In addition, I think I now have the enduring understanding that some undertakings like nails are never really finished. Teaching is that way, too. And writing. And cleaning house. And sweeping out the barn. There will always be something else that could be done. There will always be some way to make something better. There will always be something new to learn.

Anyway, you and I seem to have switched sleeping patterns. While you were an early light sleeper, I was a late heavy sleeper. So much so that I wet my bed for several years. That must have been obnoxious having to change my sheets so many times. I'm so sorry that you had to put up with that. I suppose I was too young or too groggy to even have the presence of mind to help with the bedding. For whatever reason, I have come to be just the opposite now. It might have something to do with the fact that school (my job) starts very early and I have a long drive to get there. I get up early with the animals and I find it difficult to stay up much past 9 pm. However, in the middle of the night, when the dog gets up and patiently sits by the foot of the bed, I wake up to bring him outside. He doesn't even have to bark. Meanwhile, I try not to call you before 10 am.

On those comfortable evenings in the living room, I usually sat too close to the TV. You told me over and over again to move back. It wasn't until 6th grade that I got glasses. Up until then, I was able to guess the letters pretty well on the eye test, so no one knew that the board in front of the classroom was a blur. Fortunately, I was primarily an auditory learner and would remember what was said in the classroom. And when you made me sit on the couch, I could figure out what was happening in the TV show well enough. I remember getting my first pair of glasses. When I put them on, I looked at the person standing next to me and I could see the individual hairs instead of one big mat of hair. I had no idea that it was even possible to see that clearly.

Because you worked, we could afford glasses and braces. I couldn't even bite into a sandwich properly the way my teeth protruded. And when I completely lost my front tooth in a collision with the asphalt and needed a root canal and a whole new tooth, I was taken care of. So, again, thank you.

I also appreciated how you always made sure we had someone to watch us when you were gone. I enjoyed my time with Josephine; we had tea parties with that miniature tea set. I liked walking her to the bus stop. When Grandma G died and you and Dad had to go to New York, Mrs. D stayed with us. I liked her, too. I wonder how you felt about having to leave for work or other commitments. You may have missed some special moments, like maybe my first steps. But, like me, I think you might be an introvert who needs solitude to recharge. And like me, you may have enjoyed the change of pace. I sensed that you garnered satisfaction from utilizing your skills at work. You balanced your work and home quite well. I hope you got what you needed out of both. I, too, have found an agreeable balance.

You encouraged me early on to find my own employment, or at least ways for me to volunteer or serve. I babysat when I could. I collected money for UNICEF on Halloween. I volunteered at a day camp for mentally challenged people. I tutored a Vietnamese girl in high school. In college I volunteered with the Society of St. Vincent de Paul and visited a nursing home every week. I played the accordion at the state home. And you connected me with folks who needed someone to do errands or polish silver. For many Saturdays I went to this lady's apartment and polished her silver. She gave me a few dollars for my efforts. Years later I came to understand that this was never about the silver or the money. I may have been the only person she socialized with all week. All the jobs we had, all the activities we spent our time on, all the people we met along the way, all of these things speak so much more about what we value and who we are.

k

This page is intentionally left blank.
Feel free to doodle, take notes, or just take a brain break.

2 – Challenges

Dear Mom,

Perhaps the first real challenge I met was learning to walk. I was so fat that it was assumed that I would be late reaching this milestone. We had two copper stools in the living room. Drums sort of. I remember the day I took my first step. Dad moved them farther and farther away from each other as I leaned on one and then fell toward the other. At one miraculous point, instead of just falling onto the second stool, I actually took a step or two. I walked from one stool to the other. Then Dad moved the second stool behind him and my bulbous little legs transported me to his joyous arms. I don't think I realized the significance of this event, but I do remember how happy Dad was at that moment. So I was happy, too. I haven't stopped walking since.

Thanks to you and Dad, I definitely had an enriched environment growing up. When I was less than five years old, Dad knew a Chinese exchange student and befriended his family. I remember playing in Hampton Gardens with their little girl. I don't know how much English she knew, but I do recall having fun. This was only the beginning of my fascination with people who have different customs and languages and lifestyles. In Girl Scouts, my group explored Scotland for the International Day. I remember being a little upset that we didn't chose a more exotic country, whose language used foreign characters, but I still remember the song we sang and the scones we made.

When I was in elementary school, I remember Dad trying to teach me some French. Going back and forth across the dinner table saying "tu" over and over, until I got the sound just right. I took French in high school. I even initiated the French club, which actually traveled to France when I was a junior. My first plane ride. And of course I brought you back some stamps. When my older brother came home from high school speaking Russian, he taught me three words:

Здравствуйте ('zdrav-stvoo-tye'),

Спасибо ('spah-see-bah'), and

До свидания ('duh-svee-dah-nya')

("Hello," "Thank you," and "Good Bye")   I was intrigued. I went to a different high school than my brother did, so I had to wait until college to formally study Russian. I have always remembered these three words as the first (but not the last) Russian words I learned.

Also when I was in high school, our family hosted a Japanese exchange student in the summer time. I only learned years later that the school year in Japan included these summer months. MK taught us a little Japanese and again I was intrigued.

My interest in languages and cultures never waned. And you supported me all the while. I have been to France, Japan, Russia, China, and other places. I've learned a little Japanese, French, Russian, Chinese, and a spattering of other ways to communicate. I always brought you stamps for your collection. I realized early in life that the challenge of learning a new language is not insurmountable. After all, somewhere there's a one-year old child accepting that very challenge. It just takes practice.

I was also spellbound and impressed with your proficiency at another language, shorthand. You had secret messages on little pieces of paper all around the house. I was awed by the speed at which you could record a conversation or a dictated letter. I never learned your shorthand. I wish I had, not only to be able to decipher your messages, but maybe to have a secret language between the two of us. I did, however, figure out ways to use symbols and take notes fiendishly fast. Still, you could most certainly read your notes better than I could read mine. Your typing speed and editing expertise were also remarkable. I regret that I didn't avail myself of the opportunity to benefit from your input with my various assignments and projects for school. I suppose that would have been much more likely if I didn't always wait until the last minute.

Even Morse code piqued my interest. Sometimes, when I was supposed to be in bed, I sent Morse code messages back and forth with BS across the alley. It was fairly easy for me to climb out my bedroom window and get on the roof of the porch. Sometimes, when BS wasn't available, I was content to go out there and simply look at the stars. I continued pursuing all kinds of ways to write in code. I wrote backwards notes to classmates, sometimes left-handed. I also incorporated chemistry symbols into my writing.

Thank you for enticing me with music, too. When I was about ten, you asked me if I would like to take music lessons and you asked what instrument I would be interested in. My older brother had played the accordion for years, and I liked the sound and complexity. The right hand did something completely different from the left hand. So I started taking lessons from Mr. B, who lived on the same block. Sometimes he came to the house, but I do recall occasionally lugging the accordion to his house for a lesson. Then when we bought a used piano, I started piano lessons. In high school I started learning the violin. I don't think I ever became a master at any of these instruments, but I very much enjoyed practicing.

I learned from you and Dad about the difference between a vocation and a hobby. Dad liked to draw and build things. You collected stamps and nurtured a garden. There was a period of time when I sometimes shared time with you crocheting or doing needlepoint. Not every interest has to turn into a money-making job. I was never going to make a living with music. Or with foreign languages. But my exposure to a variety of possible pastimes has given me many choices about how to spend my time. And how to challenge myself.

You exposed me to all manner of potential interests and passions, giving me the opportunity to figure out what I liked and didn't like, while equipping me with skills across the spectrum. I attended swimming lessons at the YWCA and at Marquette Park. I even remember dance lessons and recitals. My cousin and I learned about plants at the botanical gardens. We also took driving lessons together. You taught me how to play pinochle and we entered tournaments together. I took sewing and cooking in summer school. I played on softball teams. I went camping with the Girl Scouts. I was active in the Catholic Youth Council (CYC). Your support was unwavering. You bought a backstop so I could practice pitching by myself. I remember shopping for camping gear in preparation for my first overnight camping adventure. You supported my drive to earn as many Girl Scout badges as I could without getting a horse or a boat. I still clean up as I go when I cook, according to the requirements of the cooking badge. I even entered a cooking contest once. You supported me when I sold as many ads as possible for the CYC playbook. Who knew I could be so charming, persistent, persuasive, and driven? Because I sold so many ads, they created a new advertising committee that year just for the two top sellers, FS and me. You even allowed me to indulge my yearning to have pets, as long as the snakes and hamsters remained in their cages. Sorry about that time the snake got out. Besides that escape, I did take care of the habitats and learned a lot in the process. From all of these ventures, I learned how to set goals, plan, and follow through.

You supported my interest in world travel by inviting a representative to our house to talk about a training program for travel agents. This person went on and on about the benefits and opportunities the program and this occupation would bestow. At the end of the spiel, he asked for a check and a commitment then and there. We all decided that this was a little too high pressure for a program that didn't really have any guarantees for consistent employment. Since that evening, I have always been wary of high pressure, too good to be true, sales pitches.

So many challenges you and dad presented were low pressure, low risk challenges, the kind that helped me learn how to take risks and become resilient. Like the jigsaw puzzles we did on the dining room table. You brought home all types of puzzles. Some were more captivating than others. Everyone contributed at their own pace and there was no time limit, no penalty, and no prize regardless of what you did or did not accomplish. There was always a dictionary handy when we played Scrabble. We derived personal satisfaction and mutual pride from all of these challenges. We were briefly stymied by the 3-dimensional Eiffel Tower puzzle, but we eventually figured it out. Together. This also taught us teamwork. And the notion that each person's ideas were worthy of consideration. And everyone's contributions were valued.

The challenge we never did complete was the 9000 piece puzzle that you brought home. This may have been an indication of a spatial issue that we share. I have been accused of trying to stuff ten pounds into a five pound bag, attesting to my less than stellar ability to judge such things. Maybe I got that from you. The finished size of the 9000 piece puzzle may have fit on some oversized table, but the scattered pieces filled up more than 6 4'x8' pieces of plywood in the basement at last count. We never finished that puzzle. It was fun trying, though.

Dad also presented me with challenges. He once made me a pair of stilts. I'm not really sure why. Maybe he noticed that I had an excellent sense of balance because I could walk across the top of the monkey bars at the park without falling. Or maybe he just had two extra pieces of wood from a project. I remember coming home from school one Friday afternoon and seeing him on the porch with these two pieces of wood. I didn't know what they were. He told me they were stilts. I asked how to walk on them. He said he didn't know. He left them on the porch and went inside. The gauntlet was effectively thrown down. I spend that whole weekend teaching myself how to walk on those stilts. By Sunday evening, I could not only walk on those stilts, but I could also go up and down steps and curbs balancing on these two pieces of wood. The satisfaction of accomplishment was enough for me. I reveled more in this triumph than in any A I ever got on a school paper.

Teaching myself how to walk on stilts was challenging. Completing a three-dimensional puzzle was challenging. Trying to find a missing snake was challenging. Learning

Chinese or Russian or Japanese was challenging. Practicing karate was challenging. Playing the accordion was challenging. Getting an A was not. Thank you for all the stimulating challenges.

k

This page is intentionally left blank.
Would you like to doodle, take notes, or take a brain break?

3 – Walking

Dear Mom,

When I was very young, Grandma G and Aunt T came to visit us. We all walked to the snow cone stand on Watson. One of my younger siblings was still in a stroller. Later, our family walked to Dairy Queen and back on summer evenings. I have always loved walking. I walked to grade school, or I ran if I overslept. It was only a block away. I also walked the mile to and from high school. Even in college, I walked from north campus to south campus and back quite a bit. Sometimes I just walked to walk. Along railroad tracks. Around the park. When I worked at the zoo, I walked for about an hour to cover the three and a half miles one way. Once in a while, I ran late and had to take the bus. But I usually walked. I even walked to work at Catholic Supply even when the snow was two feet deep that one February. On all of our vacations, we did a lot of walking. We walked up Taum Sauk mountain; we walked along Lake Shore Drive; we walked across the Royal Gorge Bridge; we walked through the cliff dwellings at Mesa Verde; we walked in the Petrified Forest; we walked around Silver Dollar City; we walked to most of the natural springs in the state. You showed me that walking is the best mode of transportation if you really want to see the sights.

For me, walking served more than one purpose. Once in a while, when the arguments at home got unbearable, I would leave the house and walk. I needed to calm down and decompress. I would eventually return home. You worried. You worried much more for my safety than I did. I was at a party at the zoo one evening and I was not having a particularly pleasant time. I was having trouble finding someone to talk with. I started wondering if anyone would notice if I left. I didn't think so, so I left. I climbed the fence and proceeded to walk home. At about midnight. Alone. I made it past your bedroom door and all the way up the creaky stairs to bed. I was almost asleep when the phone rang. It was JT asking if I was home. When you found out I walked home, you were furious. It had taken me an hour to get home, which means that it took them that long to even notice that I wasn't there. Perhaps proving my theory.

Walking was one of my ways of dealing with awkwardness or discomfort. Since I often found myself in awkwardness, I often walked. When I was away at college, I walked along the railroad tracks outside of Atchison for hours at a time. And in Lawrence, I walked out of a party and kept walking all night until arriving at Topeka in the morning. I don't think I ever told you about this. You would have worried.

I walked to and from school in Tatsuno town in Japan and sometimes even from Tatsuno to Minamiminowa village and back instead of taking the train. I would walk around and around the park when I was memorizing *The Desiderata*. I hiked with the Girl Scouts. On a few occasions overseas, I got lost walking. I didn't need to worry you about that, either. In each case I eventually found my way back.

I wanted desperately to walk to Grandma P's house when she didn't answer her phone. You didn't permit me to go. You said it was too dangerous because there was a layer of ice on the ground. Maybe I should have told you about all the other dangerous adventures I had been on, after all. Maybe I should have gone anyway. If I did, grandma may not have had to spend three days on the floor. This is another case, I think, of how gender matters and how there are things that males can do that females cannot. After I lost the bid to go, a younger male cousin was allowed to go and only then did grandma get to the hospital. I regret not following my intuition on this day so long ago. I regret not making a stronger case. I guess I also regret not telling you more about my various escapades. Once again, you were more worried for my sake than I ever was. I appreciate now that you were just trying to keep me safe.

I feel safe when I'm walking. Grounded I guess. For me, it's easy and I can do it for long periods of time. Putting one foot in front of the other. One step at a time. Like many things in life, making progress a little at a time. Another thing I like about walking is that it doesn't matter what gender you are. Several times in my life, my options were limited because I was female. When I was in fifth grade, I thought I might like to be a priest. In school I had participated in the planning of masses and I often did the readings. I thought I might be someone people could talk to, like Fr. H is. Then I was told that women are not allowed to be priests. This made no sense to me. It still doesn't.

I joined the track team when I went to high school. JW was also on the track team, so we often walked together around the track. Another thing I like about walking is that when you are with someone, you can talk while you walk, but you don't have to bother with eye contact. Sometimes when I am listening, I look around. I'm not being rude. It actually helps me concentrate on what the other person is saying. I was only on the track team for two years. One reason is that JW was two years ahead of me and so she graduated. I wasn't very confident that I would find another track partner as wonderful as JW. But there was another reason.

I was a high jumper and a long jumper and hurdler. I was not very skilled at the running part. But I found peace and calm being on the track and sometimes my favorite part of the workout was the walk around the track to warm up or wind down. Anyway, I enjoyed the jumping, so I asked if I could try pole vaulting. High jumping with a stick. I will never forget the meeting I had with the athletic director. He told me that girls were not allowed to pole vault. When I asked for some justification, the only thing he could come up with was, "You wouldn't want muscles under your prom dress." Just wow.

So you weren't the only one who made distinctions based on gender. Perhaps it was just the societal constructs that may or may not have any basis in logic. Perhaps I should have told you about how all the challenges you provided me developed in me an ability to solve problems, think critically, and improvise beyond my years or my gender. Perhaps I should have told you about all the potentially dangerous situations that I managed to extricate myself from. Or perhaps not. I was nearly at the top of that hickory tree before anyone knew it. I don't think I knew there was anything to worry about until you freaked out a little. I slowly and carefully made it back down with no problem. One step at a time. I did not want you to worry needlessly.

I don't climb trees much anymore, but I still walk. It is my exercise of choice even now. I probably wouldn't have been very good at pole vaulting, anyway. I'm so sorry that it has become painful for you to walk. I think we shared an appreciation for the serenity that comes from a nice long stroll. I hope you have pleasant memories of all of the walks we took. I certainly do.

k

This page is intentionally left blank.
Feel free again to doodle, take notes, or just take a brain break.

4 – Cheerleader and Storage

Dear Mom,

I don't think I ever told you how truly grateful to you I am for all the support and encouragement you demonstrated through the years. You came to see me in CYC plays (*MASH* and *FLIPPED*), in a high school play (*Oliver*), and you even drove the six hours to witness my performance in the college play in Atchison (*The Mikado*). You watched my performance as the Mother Abbess (*The Sound of Music*) at a local parish. I appreciated your being there when you could. I knew you were very busy. Even when you couldn't quite make it, you have always been my most steadfast cheerleader. You tell everyone who will listen about all my accomplishments. You came to my high school graduation. I know you were very proud of me being the valedictorian. I wonder if you were disappointed that your valedictorian daughter was not invited to make any kind of speech. Oh well.

I could count on you to spread the word about all my travels. You always had a map out to show where I was. France, Japan, Russia, China, and several points in between. Even though you were skeptical about me spending my savings to visit the Missionary of Charities

Convent in New York over Christmas break, I suspect you might have been secretly proud of me even then.

You positively beamed with all my degrees and certifications. All the jobs I had. And most recently all of my animal exploits. I feel like you are my personal publicity agent. You clearly wanted to be a part of my life and you undoubtedly are. I'm sorry if I didn't express my gratitude more consistently. Everywhere I went, I was thinking of you and looking for the perfect memento to bring back for you.

Fortunately, all the while I was wandering around the world, you graciously let me keep all of my stuff at your house. I admit that for many years I was a hoarder. I wonder where I got that from. Maybe DNA played a part in this. I certainly had relatives who collected. Dad collected books, magazines, tools. You collected stamps, puzzles, and salt and pepper shakers. From early on, I was fascinated with oil lamps and tea pots and spoons. And Aunt T, of course, collected absolutely everything.

I sometimes saw benefits of having collections. Every time I was curious about something new, Dad was able to say, "Oh yes, I have a book about that in the basement." Since I had a fascination with languages, there was always an interesting stamp that needed to be translated. And, you must admit, it is convenient to have an oil lamp in case the power goes out. And you never know when you will need a button extender. Additionally, it is easier to choose gifts for someone who has a collection.

I learned from you how to collect and organize photos. I remember watching in our living room the slide shows of vacations or special events. And when photos came back from being developed, I watched you carefully label and date each photo and create countless memory albums. I observed and understood early on that this level of organization takes time and effort. I have photo albums for all the various phases in my life. I may not have been as meticulous in my labeling, but I do have quite an extensive assortment of pictures. I do find it quite fascinating, though, how you can manage more often than not to close your eyes just as the shutter clicks.

You and I have always had different methods for storing and organizing. You used file cabinets. I was more of a pile or box person, like dad I guess. I do generally have a label on each box. Later, after years of teaching, I found myself trying to translate for parents who file and students who pile. Communication can be difficult when organizational styles clash.

I imagine that you would find it somewhat amusing to know that one of my favorite college jobs was housekeeping. You were always trying to get me to clean my room. I actually did keep my room fairly clean. But I don't think I have ever been good at organizing my room, or more precisely, organizing all my stuff. I think there is a distinction between cleaning and organizing. I did, however, find it tremendously satisfying to clean someone else's room. What I particularly enjoyed about my housekeeping jobs is that I could tell when I was finished:

the trash cans were empty, the surfaces were dusted, the floor was vacuumed. In my own room and in my own house, the work of cleaning and even organizing is never finished. I really do like my label maker, though. I'll keep working on it.

k

This page is intentionally left blank,
in case you want to doodle, take notes, or just take a brain break.

5 – Food

Dear Mom,

Between the fresh vegetables and berries from the garden and all of your recipes, we did eat well. You put in long hours in the back yard garden, and the dinner table was richer for it. I've always liked the variety of vegetables we had for dinner. The only food you served that I could not stomach (and still can't) was the liver. You got delicious local catfish from someone at work. And once in a while, a neighbor gave us farm fresh eggs. I'm grateful for the early exposure to such an assortment of healthy flavors. I'm sure this helped me adjust to the international cuisine when I traveled.

I loved chemistry, and cooking is basically chemistry. I enjoyed trying new combinations and recipes. Judging from all the notes on your recipe cards, so did you. Thank you very much, by the way, for later lending me your recipes, especially the recipes for all those Christmas cookies we grew up with.

Our family boasted a rich and flavorful holiday feast tradition. We started baking Christmas cookies in October and froze many batches, so we would have enough for gift boxes and for the holiday get-togethers. Batches and batches of cookies were in the basement freezer for months. I wonder if you knew that I occasionally raided that stash a few cookies at a time. Yum.

We also had delicious Thanksgiving meals. We probably didn't let you know enough how much we appreciated your efforts. I particularly liked your sweet potato dish with lots of marshmallows. And that broccoli cheese casserole. Through the years, I altered that recipe so much that I just called it broccoli surprise. You never knew what secret ingredients I might add. I also reveled in the times I spent learning the fine art of pie making from dad. I got to be pretty good at making pies. For my birthday celebrations, I preferred pie to cake. Still do.

The whole family went out to eat at the restaurant chosen by the one whose birthday we were celebrating. We all had different preferences, which was perfectly fine. Being different was okay in our family. You honored and respected our uniqueness. And we learned to accept and encourage individuality in others. I embraced this when I traveled and when I taught.

Nevertheless, I missed those cookies and pies when I lived in Japan. Thanks for sending me copies of your recipes. I was able to bring the Christmas cookie tradition to a whole different country. (In Japan, they had a Christmas cake tradition, which included Christmas cake parties. But no one had cookies like yours.) I also improvised sometimes. You showed me that cooking is experimentation, so that's what I did. In my village, they had plenty of pumpkins, used for soups and sides, but I introduced a pumpkin pie that I made from scratch (from memory) and it was well received. Because of your guidance, I am now able to take almost any ingredients and make a meal. Or a dessert. You brought home a yogurt maker once, and we all enjoyed homemade yogurt, trying all different flavors. I also experimented in my room. In test tubes, I successfully made a tasty peach wine. I tried to grow apple trees, but that didn't work out so well.

One of these days, I will organize all of these wonderful recipes you shared with me and all the recipes I have encountered on my own. You had all of them in categories on cards in a box. Mine are in a box, too, but it's basically just a pile of papers and cards. It's on my list of things to do.

Meanwhile, though, I maintain a farm, where I have my own free-range chickens and ducks and they provide me with a generous supply of fresh and healthy eggs. I don't have a garden yet; I would need to figure out how to set it up so that the goats, chickens, and ducks don't mess with the crop. That's also on my list of things to do. I do have batches of fescue growing here and there that the goats, ducks, and chickens feast on. This has also been an experiment; I throw out seeds and see what takes. I'm glad I have enough eggs to not only donate to the local pantry but also to give to you to distribute at your place. You were always superb at figuring out what people needed and filling that need, whether it be school project supplies, camping equipment, recipes, or farm fresh eggs.

k

This page is intentionally left blank.
Here's another opportunity to doodle, take notes, or just take a brain break.

6 – Stories and Movies

Dear Mom,

I love listening to your stories. When we took the bus to the Cardinal games, you told us about going to the games with your mom years ago. And speaking of the bus, I was particularly moved by the story of when a group of your friends were going somewhere and they wouldn't let one of the friends on the bus because she was not Caucasian. I was proud of the fact that you didn't leave that friend behind.

You and Dad talked about when you were dating. You met at a dance sponsored by the USO. The United Service Organizations strengthen America's military service members by keeping them connected to family, home, and country. Dad was in the Air Force, stationed nearby, and he would take the bus to your house from the downtown YMCA where he sometimes stayed or maybe even back and forth from the Air Force base. You went to England by boat to marry Dad after he was transferred there. I remember you saying that your younger sisters were waiting for you, the oldest, to marry so that they could proceed with their own life plans.

Do you remember the story about one of your childhood Christmases, the one when your electricity went out? Christmas was saved at the last minute by a kind stranger. (I recounted that story for a school assignment. The teacher marked me down because she didn't believe that it was a non-fiction story as assigned. I'll never forget that.) We both have had run ins with kind strangers. I got my belief in the goodness of humanity from you and Dad.

One time, when I and a friend were on the way to college friend's wedding, we ran out of gas and were forced to stop on the highway about a half mile from the next exit. We walked to the exit and got the gas can and gas from the store. The clerk at the store lent us her car keys so that I could drive back to the car. That was so nice and trusting of her. I still believe in the kindness of strangers.

When I walked to Topeka from Lawrence, I was cold and wet and tired when I got to Topeka in the morning. A stranger helped me dry off, take a nap, and get back to where I was supposed to be.

I enjoyed the times when we escaped from friends and strangers alike to see a movie together. We saw *National Velvet*, *Ben Hur*, *Lost Horizon*, and *Pinocchio*, among other classics. Those were precious times when I had you to myself. You and Dad were wonderful about giving each of us our own space and our own times apart from each other. This is difficult to accomplish when you have four children.

Some of the stories you told about me were of things I do not remember. Like the time I tried to feed a leaf to a very big dog and the dog bit my face instead. Or the first time I threw up and I thought I was dying because I believed that I was losing all of my insides. Or the phase I went through when I held my breath if I was frustrated. You told me that it was a little scary because sometimes I could hold my breath for quite a long time. I love hearing all these stories. I wish I had written all of them down.

k

This page is intentionally left blank.
I welcome you, one more time, to doodle, take notes, or just take a brain break.

7 – Two Peas in a Pod

Dear Mom,

Like it or not, many of my habits and idiosyncrasies are clearly influenced by you. I destroy the name and address on any envelope or paper I throw away. I write the dates, check number, and amount on a bill, a practice reinforced at some of my many jobs. I document, document, document, keeping records of transactions so that I can refer to names and dates and even quotes if need be. This saved me lots of money over the years from unscrupulous people and companies that counted on the possibility that I did not keep track of such specifics. I think I got my attention to detail from both you and Dad, as well as my propensity to automatically edit whatever I see. I got my thick hair from you, definitely. And probably my not so good teeth. We're both excellent spellers. And there is always a nail file nearby.

I guess we also share passion and enthusiasm which may have been why we clashed so much when I was in high school. I don't really remember what we argued about. I do remember leaving the house sometimes when things got too loud or contentious. Sometimes you didn't hear me and sometimes I didn't hear you. I have learned since then that sometimes we only hear what we are ready to hear. I would walk and walk for hours just to clear my head. Sometimes just around the park. Sometimes farther away. Then when I returned you would be angry that I left. You said it was dangerous. I remember saying that I couldn't imagine anyone waiting behind a bush for some silly teenager to walk by. I remember thinking that if my friend and classmate can be killed in her own kitchen, "How does my safety really depend upon where I walk?" I had a hard time with this.

The Nicolette Larson song expressed how I felt. *It's gonna take a lotta love to change the way things are. It's gonna take a lotta love or we won't get too far. So if you look in my direction and we don't see eye to eye, my heart needs protection and so do I.* Apparently, there was a lot of love there, because we got through those rough patches.

I suppose I needed time away to figure things out and learn even more about life and about myself. My various jobs and the opportunity to make time and a half, often interfered with my ability or willingness to come home for the holidays. So did my Come And See visit with the Missionaries of Charity in New York. I guess this is one of those temporarily unpleasant side-effects of modeling and teaching independence. I cherish the memories of our family traditions, like when we all went for a drive to see the lights and came back to dad saying Santa had visited while we were gone. Again!?! But I was compelled to explore other options. I did often bring a little home with me wherever I went, like when I made your cookies in

Japan or when I made myself a new pair of stilts at college. Still, I imagine it is a little heart wrenching when the birds leave the nest and spread their wings. I wish I was better at conveying to you how well you had prepared me for this exploration beyond the nest.

I learned from you that doing a little at a time can add up. Whenever you walked up the stairs, you picked up a piece or two of lint off the carpet. This left less to clean on cleaning day. I apply this to many of my big tasks. If I can't dedicate a whole day to something, I do a piece at a time whenever I can. In my classroom I am able to chunk the work for my students, sometimes in a way that surprises them when they see their completed work. Filling one water pail at a time. Losing one pound at a time. Walking one mile at a time. Taking one class at a time. Clearing one branch at a time on my property. Like you pulled one weed at a time in your garden. Eventually much is accomplished.

Another thing I shared with you was the occasional inclination toward more thoughtful, philosophical discussions. I wonder if I partly got the idea for the US group from your discussion club. You and Dad met with other couples and eventually socialized with the families often. I remember the 4th of July tradition when all these families converged at a member's house for a day of games, food, and fireworks. In high school, I started the US group, which gathered regularly to explore weighty topics. Maybe subconsciously, I was trying to follow in your footsteps.

We both have thoroughly enjoyed exploring the world through travel. I share your fascination and respect for people who are different from us. I, like you, tend to ask questions rather than jump to conclusions. I know, because of you, how to stand up for myself and how to stand up for others. I, like you, do not judge people according to stereotypes or characteristics they can't control.

Of course, we have our differences. You drink coffee; I prefer tea. You like liver; I hate liver. I like corn; you are not a fan of corn. I remember when we had liver, you wouldn't let me watch TV until I finished it. Yuk. I don't know if I ever finished the liver. I may have settled for just listening to *The Six Million Dollar Man* from the dining room. I was a night owl and you were early to bed, early to rise. And now this is reversed. You wear make-up and I don't. You have a sense of fashion; I do not. I take great pleasure in all manner of creatures on the farm; you, not so much. That's okay. If we were all the same, what a boring world this would be!

I'm gratified that you feel comfortable talking with me about topics other people tend to avoid. We both have somewhat of a matter-of-fact approach to things, things like finances, death, medicine, pain. As you say, "It is what it is." I think you have helped me become comfortable with the reality where there are things we can control and there are things we cannot control. And we do the best we can possibly do with what we have.

k

This page is intentionally left blank.
Feel free to doodle, take notes, or just take a brain break.

8 – I'm Ready

Dear Mom,

Have I told you about all of the times when I could have died? I've had adventures, some of which could easily have resulted in something horrible. I suppose that traveling as much as I did comes with risks. And since I never minded traveling alone and being somewhat anonymous, I had a propensity to wander. I liked disappearing into the crowd. In Rome, I reveled in my solo dinner at that mountaintop restaurant when I requested a French-speaking waiter. I was thrilled when a shopkeeper in Paris assumed I was from Quebec because of my accent. No one knew me. No one had preconceptions of me based on my history or background. Thus the rewards of travel. Every once in a while, I like to immerse myself in a foreign situation and reinvent myself. If only for a while. Again, I was hiding in plain sight.

I was a little nervous, though, when that guy seemed to be following me through the streets of Paris to the Eiffel Tower. Apparently my invisibility cloak had a few holes. I was alone in Paris. I seemed to have escaped this stalker when I ascended the tower. (Maybe this distraction made me forget to restock my film before going up.) I guess I did elude him, or perhaps there wasn't anything to fret about in the first place. In any case, he was nowhere to be seen when I came back down quite a while later.

Then on that same day, I momentarily panicked because the station name my host dad gave me did not match any of the options on the metro. It could have ended badly if I hadn't calmed down and somehow remembered enough of a previous French conversation when he told me about a name change in his village.

And a few weeks before that, I had wandered a little too far from the hotel in Tours, so much so that I did not know how to get back. I wandered some more, and eventually found my way.

Perhaps I can't blame this entirely on traveling. I got into plenty of precarious situations closer to home. One memorable example was when my car spun and spun on highway 40 on ice when I almost missed the Hanley exit and overcompensated. I might have died then and there. Amazingly, though there was no logical reason for this, no cars happened to be on the highway in those few minutes. I had the whole expanse to myself. When I stopped spinning and was facing the wrong direction on the multilane highway, I considered myself wildly lucky or inexplicably blessed.

And the car fires. Oh yes, the multiple car fires. The first time was when the brakes collapsed into the tire as I was travelling at 70 mph in the left lane on a July Saturday afternoon. That rubber fire burned through to the back seat before the fire truck finally arrived on the scene. After this

I remember thinking I should get a fire extinguisher for my car. I also remember some folks saying that I shouldn't bother because "What are the chances that this will happen again?" Lightning surely doesn't strike twice. I bought a fire extinguisher anyway. I also had to find another car.

A friend had an old car in a barn he hadn't used in many months. So I went to see it. We even had to find a battery for it. When it started right away, I called it Lazarus. On the way home in Lazarus, one of the tires blew. Amazingly, there was a spare and a tire iron in the trunk. This is when EH showed me how to change a tire. Good thing because later, on the way to Ohio alone, on the Indiana-Ohio border, my right rear tire went flat. I changed the tire by myself. It was about 11 pm. A passing car could easily have taken me out. It seems I did a lot of my best work late at night.

Anyway, pulling into Dayton, I saw another car on fire. So I stopped like a good Samaritan and put the fire out with my new extinguisher. I got out of there when I smelled alcohol on the other driver's breath. Then when I got to my destination and filled up at the gas station, smoke started coming out from under my hood. Well, the extinguisher was empty from helping that drunk guy, so I had to run into the store to get theirs. The most astounding part of this whole experience is that several minutes after my request, the clerk and the folks in line did not seem to comprehend the urgency of a car on fire at the gas pump. Wow. At any of these moments, it could have been appallingly disastrous. But it wasn't. The most I got out of each of these incidents was a good story and a life lesson. And mounting evidence that maybe I could figure stuff out okay. Or maybe I was just very, very lucky.

And then there was the time I played a double header softball game and ended up in the hospital with a temperature of 104 degrees. Like you, my normal temperature is closer to 96 than 98.6, so a 104 was potentially devastating. Fortunately, when I started ranting incoherently, my friends had sense enough to get me to the hospital right away where they packed all my pressure points with ice for what seemed like hours until my temperature approached a safe level. It was very dark when I left the hospital. I could have died. I hadn't stayed hydrated and I pitched both games. And it was hot. I wasn't even sweating anymore.

When I was living in Topeka, one time I got the stomach flu, or I think that's what it was. I was too sick to even get out of bed much. And I had a fever for several days. Because I didn't show up for work, BJ and KR were caring and thoughtful enough to check on me. When they did, they discovered that my apartment was boiling hot. Something I had not noticed because my own temperature was so high. They opened windows, turned on fans, and filled the bath with cool water. These were my lean college days. I didn't have a doctor or any kind of health plan.

When I went to visit a friend in Omaha, I bit into some spun honey and suddenly found myself chewing on what used to be my false front tooth. So when I had to get the tooth replaced, I made payments to the dentist for quite a while. Fortunately the hospital took payments over time, too.

Another Topeka story involved some dogs and a guy with a knife. I was living with a friend and her dogs, working, and taking some classes at the college. We were sitting by the bay window one evening when the dogs started to bark ferociously, moving from one window to another. After the dogs finally stopped barking, we looked around and noticed that one of the window screens had been cut on three of the four sides. When the guy kept showing up, usually right after we both got home, our friends took turns staying with us. This went on for several weeks. Eventually a police helicopter circled in search of this guy. That may have been enough to scare him off. He never returned, but it was sure nice to have those dogs and those friends. I don't know if I ever told you this, either. There wasn't much you could have done long distance, except be anxious, I guess.

Also in Topeka, when I was working at the Kwik Shop, I started bleeding continuously. I mean really bleeding. Like a freely flowing river. More blood than I had ever seen at once. I hadn't fallen. I hadn't been hit. I hadn't even lifted anything heavy. I called the person who was supposed to work the next shift, asking him to hurry. Before my relief got there, I fainted into the arms of one of the regular customers, weak from having lost so much blood. I was able to call GS and he came and took me to the hospital just as my relief arrived. One of my arteries had ruptured and needed to be cauterized.

Did I ever tell you about the time I was on a float trip and took one too many steps away from the fire? I tumbled several yards straight down into the river. I don't know how I didn't lose my glasses. Did I tell you about the tornado in Atchison when I ran across campus under the green clouds to get candles from the chapel? Did I tell you about the time I almost cut my thumb off on cardboard when I was packing boxes in Japan? Or the time I smashed my thumb in the door of a skyline car in China? It's very fortunate that you had me take CPR and first aid classes. Most of the time, as it turns out, I put this knowledge to good use for myself.

I don't even know if I told you about any of this. I didn't want to worry you or it just never came up. After my apartment was broken into, I remember you telling me that I should ask for help when I need it. It, quite honestly, had not occurred to me that I should bother other people with my trials and tribulations. I thought that I was asserting my independence. I have since learned that it is not weakness to seek and receive help from others. This was, and still is sometimes, a tricky concept for me to grasp. I'm not adept at asking for what I need or sharing troubles. I may have gotten that partially from you, you know. I don't remember you letting me know when you were going to have your gall bladder removed. I only learned about it after the fact. I guess you didn't want to worry me, either.

Meanwhile, there were moments when I thought that I could die happy. After the trip to France in high school, I thought that I had reached the pinnacle. I couldn't imagine what could be better. Years later when I sang that duet with Minami Kosetsu at the sushi restaurant in Nashville, I would have been content with going out on that high note.

But there were always more pinnacles just over the horizon. With every goal that I met, there was something else I wanted to try. And I suppose God just wasn't quite ready for me when I was 17 or 33. I've done a lot of neat things, and I have relished telling you some of these stories.

I wish there would be a lot less pain, though. I'm glad I don't remember much from my hospital stay with that bladder infection. I do remember kneeling on a piece of glass in center field and feeling that for several long weeks. I also remember vividly the obnoxious, regular pain I had every month for more than three decades. At least I knew that it would subside in four or five days, but it was still obnoxious. And I didn't think I could endure the bursting of those cysts or the cystectomy that followed. Especially since I had no idea how long that pain would last. Sometimes, there are no pills strong enough. It's unfortunate, one might agree, that we haven't yet developed the means to transfer our consciousness into a cyborg body. But for now, it is what it is.

Nevertheless, I would like to think that our consciousness persists. I am comfortable in the belief that the grandmas and grandpas, your sister, and my dad are all watching us and having a good chuckle now and then.

As long as we are still here, there will always be something on my to do list, always a new challenge to undertake, always something new to learn, always more questions to ask, always more pastries to eat, always another story to share, always more eggs to distribute, always more books to write.

k

This page is intentionally left blank.
Feel free to doodle, take notes, or just take a brain break.

About the Author

Kateri is a writer: passionately, incessantly, fervently, and now publicly.

Whether in the form of backwards notes to classmates, stream of consciousness journaling, letters to pen pals, handouts for presentations, letters of recommendation, or her doctoral thesis, she has been writing most of her life.

She tries to balance this with spending time with her animals and other family members, walking, and solving increasingly more difficult Sudokus.

Made in the USA
San Bernardino, CA
24 July 2017